BRINGING THE CHURCH INTO COMMUNITY:

8 COMPONENTS TO COMMUNITY DEVELOPMENT

Daniel Mottayaw
Author

This book is dedicated to my beautiful fiancée, Erin Leigh Wilkinson, who taught me everything I know about community development. Thank you for allowing your passion to be contagious.

TABLE OF CONTENTS

6 Lessons on Community Development

LEADER INSTRUCTIONS

Welcome, leader! You are about to embark on the liberating journey of bringing your church into your community. But first, there are some things that need to be explained.

Target Audience

This curriculum is targeted toward young adults. Why? This is typically the age group that steps up and moves into action within the church. This is an action-oriented curriculum. If there is no action then this curriculum will fail.

Preparation

There are three headings at the beginning of each lesson: Curriculum Goal, Lesson Goal, and Prep. Read each of these sections before each lesson, and they will instruct you in how to go about preparing for the lesson. Challenge yourself to use outside "study helps." Read commentaries on the Bible passages, do word studies on interesting/important words, etc.

Teaching

Everything after the first three headings will be your "teaching material." Feel free to read what is written word-for-word, or adapt the text to best fit your style of teaching. The questions that are in bold on the "Leader Guide" are meant to be discussion questions. The learners will each receive a "Learner Guide," which is meant to be a simple memory/dialogue aid. There is space for them to write thoughts that they wish to remember, or questions that lead to conversation.

Be Open to Learning

It is impossible to completely know how to "do" community development. This curriculum has been set up in a way that the leader and learner will both benefit and be challenged to live a life that is a little closer to that of the savior: Jesus Christ.

If you keep these things in mind then you will be able to effectively walk through this journey with others, and you will discover something incredible: God desires for the Church to be brought into its surrounding communities!

Lesson 1—Leader Guide

CHURCH IN COMMUNITY

Curriculum Goal

Learners will see the importance of the local church deeply rooting themselves into the surrounding community, which will compel the learner to affectively root themselves in relationships with those around them—whether they are a part of the church or not.

Lesson Goals

- Understand how Christ restored human relationships
- Understand the basics of the eight components of community development
- Critically think about the importance of the local church rooting itself in the surrounding community

Prep (Do in order)

___ Complete Leader Guide—Use "Instructions for the Leader" as a guide
___ Print one "Learner Guide" for each person
___ Bring writing utensils for learners to use
___ Bring your Bible
___ Pray every day about how God can use you in community development
___ Find a location to meet (coffee shop, house) in the neighborhood near your church
___ Prepare an order for your gathering—Feel free to add worship music, prayer, food, etc.

How did we get here?

Churches are, at times, like college football games. Many people from all over the surrounding community gather at their team's stadium early in the morning each weekend. These people are called "fans." These fans will eat some pregame food and talk about football strategy for the upcoming game, all while wearing the proper clothing to match who they are rooting for (you don't want to wear the wrong color!). Not too long before the game starts the fans will make their way over to the stadium to find their assigned seats (many of which hold season tickets for every home game). The fans begin to file into the stadium as kick-off approaches and as excitement builds. As soon as the ball is kicked the fans are free to cheer as they wish. Some are boisterous. Some are melancholy. Some wear too much body paint. More often than not the home team ends up winning, and all the fans leave feeling satisfied and joyful heading into the next workweek. Sometimes, however, the home team loses. Fans leave upset and frustrated with their team. But, regardless of the outcome, fans will continue to show up, pay the entry fee, and cheer for their team.

Can you see how college football games can be like our churches? Churches, in many cases, have the tendency to be inward focused and event oriented. There are many benefits of this, but there are also some consequences.

What might be some of the consequences of a church being inward focused and event oriented?
Write here...

What does God say?
Read Isaiah 58:1-12
What characterizes the false fast?
Write here...

What characterizes the true fast?
Write here...

Is the true fast inward or outward focused? How can you tell?
Write here...

What does this teach us about God's character?
Write here...

Read Luke 4:16-21 (Read Luke 4 for context) (Look especially at The Message)
What was Jesus anointed to do?
Write here...

What is the year of the Lord's favor? What is the response to living in the year of the Lord's favor?
Write here...

Was Jesus inward or outward focused? How can you tell?
Write here...

What does this teach us about Jesus' character?
Write here...

What can we do?

When churches are inward focused and event oriented they are not participating in the lives of the people in their neighborhood. Instead, they are asking the people of the community to participate in their church. It is not bad to ask people to participate in the church community, but all throughout scripture we see God approaching the people first. God invades the lives of people, meets them where they are, and invites them into a reciprocating relationship.

The neighborhoods around us are hurting—even our church neighborhoods are hurting! We desire to help people in our neighborhood, but we tend to believe that we are helping by inviting them to our church. But what if we could do something different? What if there were things that we could do that help more than they hurt? Maybe there is a different way.

8 Key Components of Christian Community Development

People have been working to restore and build relationships between individuals and within communities for years. There are components that have been developed by people who have rooted themselves in the communities with the intention of helping those who are poor (understanding that poor may not always relate with monetary wealth). These are called the "8 Key Components of Christian Community Development," and come from the Christian Community Development Association (CCDA). These components have come about through practice, failing, succeeding, and constant prayer and guidance through the Holy Spirit. These components are designed to do exactly what we are talking about: Bringing the Church into community.

- **Relocation**—Living among the people with a desire for the neighbors just as much as there is a desire for self (physical and/or mental relocation)
- **Reconciliation**—Reconciling and enacting love to God and others
- **Redistribution**—Using skills and resources for the good of the community
- **Leadership Development**—Building up leaders who can help sustain the community
- **Listening to the Community**—Understanding what it is that the community desires
- **Church-Based**—A nurturing community of faith to push growth in God
- **Wholistic Approach**—Keeping the balance between growth in God and personal/community development
- **Empowerment**—Empowering others to help themselves after being helped

Briefly answer how these 8 Key Components of Christian Community Development can help churches root themselves in their neighborhoods.

Write here...

How can we do it?

However, It is not enough for us to simply have an understanding of these components. We must be implementing them in our lives. Somehow, we must take what we have learned and make that knowledge a part of what we do. So, how can we do it? How can we exercise these 8 Key Components of Christian Community Development?

In the coming lessons we will be coming up with a measurable, attainable, specific, time-oriented goals (M.A.S.T. goal) that implement the knowledge of these components into actions. For this lesson, take time to answer these two questions: 1) What is the purpose of Christian Community Development? 2) What is one specific example of Christian Community Development that you have seen in your neighborhood?

Write here...

One Sample Definition of Christian Community Development:
Christian Community Development is a means of building up a community to be a self-sustaining group of people who love God and each other selflessly.

What are others saying?

Read what NAME says in, *An Introduction to Community Development*, about the quality of life that Jesus is trying to restore:

> "Quality of life is a vague notion, and, therefore, each community must define indicators in order to be able to monitor whether or not improvement is occurring. Quality of life can refer to economic, social, psychological, physical, and political aspects of a community. Examples of indicators include: number of violent crimes within a neighborhood; hours of work at the median wage required to support basic needs' percentage of employment concentrated in the top 10 employers; percentage of the population that gardens; and tons of solid waste generated and recycled per person."

Jesus desires his people to experience a quality of life that is above what many people in communities currently experience.

Notes from Pastor/Community Developer

Take everything that you have studied throughout this lesson up to this point and discuss it with a pastor or community developer. These notes may be helpful for understanding and teaching this lesson, so write them down!

Notes:

_____
_____
_____
_____
_____
_____
_____
_____
_____

Notes from Article

Find an article from a magazine, newspaper, online journal, or even a book that relates to the topic of this lesson. These outside sources may offer other insight not received within this curriculum. These notes may be helpful for understanding and teaching this lesson, so write them down!

Notes:

_____
_____
_____
_____
_____
_____
_____
_____
_____

Statement of Belief

If you could only use one sentence to teach this lesson, what would you say?

_____
_____
_____

CHURCH IN COMMUNITY

How did we get here?

Churches are like football games at times. What might be some of the consequences of a church being inward focused and event oriented?

Discussion Notes

What does God say?

Isaiah 58:1-12
Luke 4:16-21

Discussion Notes

What can we do?

8 Key Components of Christian Community Development

Discussion Notes

How can we do it?

Answer these two questions: 1) What is the purpose of Christian Community Development? 2) What is one specific example of Christian Community Development that you have seen in your neighborhood?

Discussion Notes

"Quality of life is a vague notion, and, therefore, each community must define indicators in order to be able to monitor whether or not improvement is occurring. Quality of life can refer to economic, social, psychological, physical, and political aspects of a community."—*An Introduction to Community Development*

Lesson 2—Leader Guide

THREE "R" WORDS

Curriculum Goal

Learners will see the importance of the local church deeply rooting themselves into the surrounding community, which will compel the learner to affectively root themselves in relationships with those around them—whether they are a part of the church or not.

Lesson Goals

- The learner will understand the importance of being involved with the local community on a consistent basis
- The learner will understand the three main development components
- The learner will challenge themselves in specific ways to get involved with the local community on a consistent basis

Prep (Do in order)

___ Complete Leader Guide—Use "Instructions for the Leader" as a guide
___ Print one "Learner Guide" for each person
___ Bring writing utensils for learners to use
___ Bring your Bible
___ Pray every day about how God can use you in community development
___ Find a location to meet (coffee shop, house) in the neighborhood near your church
___ Prepare an order for your gathering—Feel free to add worship music, prayer, food, etc.

How did we get here?

We have a problem. We have a big problem. America, as most of us know it, has always been a land of distinctiveness. People from every continent fill this country. People from thousands of different religions and cults call this home. There are people who are farmers, artists, construction workers, businessmen, clergy, doctors, social workers... almost every job you can think of America can teach you to do! So, what is the problem? Among all of this distinctiveness we find individualism. Individualism is a main vein that runs through this body called,

"America." This individualism has many positives to it: personal drive, living independently, self-efficiency, and more. And that is exactly the problem! We are a personal, independent, self-sufficient, closed off society that struggles to enter into relationship with others. When we hear the Bible say, "Love your neighbor as yourself," we immediately justify who exactly are our neighbors—who we have to love, and whom we don't have to love. This causes our relationships with others to be broken and marred. And when we have broken and marred relationships with others then we cannot truly be the body of Christ that God desires to work together in perfect harmony.

Why is *individualism* a problem among communities of people?
Write here…

What does God say?
Read John 1:1-18
What is the Word? What is the Light?
Write here…

What can we learn from V. 14 when it says, "And the Word became flesh and dwelt among us?"
Write here…

What can we learn about God through this passage?
Write here…

Read Matthew 22:34-40 (Read Matthew 22 for context)
What are the two greatest commandments that Jesus states?
Write here…

Why might Jesus say that these are the two greatest commandments?
Write here…

What can we learn about God's character through this passage?
Write here...

Read Acts 2:42-47 (Read Acts 1-2 for context)
What are some of the things that the people are doing together?
Write here...

What are some of the things that the people are doing for each other?
Write here...

What can we learn about God's desire for humanity from this passage?
Write here...

What can we do?

Each week we turn our focus to the 8 Key Components of Christian Community Development in order to answer the question, "What can we do?" This week we will focus on three of those components: Relocation, Reconciliation, and Redistribution.

Relocation

As we saw in the first scripture passage from John 1, when Jesus came to the earth he lived among the people. He came as a human and fully entrenched his life within the lives of others. This goes against most of everything we see in our American culture. There is no real teaching in America that individualism is the best way to live life, but the way our society is set up communicates the idea that life is best lived as a self-sufficient individual. This is not the message that Jesus communicates by his actions. His actions say that he cares about the lives of others. His actions say that he wants to serve others before he serves himself. He located himself in places where he could come into contact with others and build meaningful and redemptive relationships with others. Jesus' actions communicate that we should not be focused just on our families, or ourselves, but that we should relocate our focus to serving the neighborhood around us. That is the first component: relocation.

Reconciliation

In the second scripture passage Jesus is giving the two greatest commands: Loving God and loving neighbor as self. This is what the second component, reconciliation, is all about. Once we have placed our focus on our neighborhood and those that surround us then we are to love them as we love ourselves. In the midst of these loving relationships with our neighbors a love of God should arise from our neighbors and us. A lot of hurt is caused in this world because of a lack of love of neighbor. Not only are we called to love our neighbors and neighborhood in all situations, but also we may be the only image of Jesus that they see throughout their day/week/month/year. This does not mean that we are the perfect Christians (we must be continually reconciling with God, too), but we can show the love of Christ through relocation and reconciliation (loving God and loving neighbor as self).

Redistribution

In the third scripture passage we see an early Christian community distributing possessions among one another. This is done to such an extreme that there were no longer any needs among the people. This touches on the third component: redistribution. Redistribution can focus on the exchange of needs (food, shelter, clothing, etc.), but it mainly focuses on the redistribution of assets. What is an asset? An asset is any skill or resource that a person has that holds some form of value. This could be an ability to speak multiple languages, owning a lawn mower, or even a teenager who is great at watching kids. When a community focuses on how to effectively redistribute the assets that a community possesses then many of the desires of the community are brought into fruition. Take the bi-lingual person for example. There may be many Spanish-speaking parents in the community that are having a hard time learning English. They desire to learn English because it will make life a lot easier in an American city. If this bi-lingual person could offer free/cheap classes then the desires of these people will come to fruition. Redistribution ultimately is a result of relocating our focus to our neighbors and neighborhoods, reconciling with those relationships around us, and taking thoughtful and loving action with the assets that we posses.

Briefly summarize relocation, reconciliation, and redistribution.

Write here...

How can we do it?

However, It is not enough for us to simply have an understanding of these components. We must be implementing them in our lives. Somehow, we must take what we have learned and make that knowledge a part of what we do. So, how can we do it? How can we relocate, reconcile, and redistribute?

Come up with a measurable, attainable, specific, time-oriented goal (M.A.S.T. goal) that implements the knowledge of these three components into actions
Write here...

One Example:
I will use my neighborhood grocery store at least half of the time for the next full year instead of traveling a further distance to larger, more inexpensive supermarket. In doing this I will begin to develop a relationship with the owners and workers of the grocery store, I will be supporting their "small-scale" business, and I will be using the resources that I have (money) to provide income (grocery store's desire) for those who work at the grocery store. My efforts may not be huge, but they are a consistent action that relocates my focus, gives me opportunity to reconcile my relationships with those in my neighborhood, and redistributes my resources to help fulfill the desires of my neighbors.

What are others saying?

Read what Overflow Church (Benton Harbor, MI) has to say about community involvement:

> "Overflow Church serves the community through multiple efforts... [Overflow] church... supports the local women's safe shelter in practical ways and by loving the people who find safety there... hosts two summer Vacation Bible Schools in areas that are primarily under-resourced, promotes, invites and hosts mission teams to partner with the church to provide practical needs in the community such as home repair and painting neighborhood houses, looks to work with the community and create collaborative efforts and help individuals find places to serve, [and] has a growing street ministry in Benton Harbor."

They are a phenomenal example of relocating into the community, reconciling with God the people that live in their community, and redistributing the resources and assets within the community.

Notes from Pastor/Community Developer

Take everything that you have studied throughout this lesson up to this point and discuss it with a pastor or community developer. These notes may be helpful for understanding and teaching this lesson, so write them down!

Notes:

_____
_____
_____
_____
_____
_____
_____
_____
_____

Notes from Article

Find an article from a magazine, newspaper, online journal, or even a book that relates to the topic of this lesson. These outside sources may offer other insight not received within this curriculum. These notes may be helpful for understanding and teaching this lesson, so write them down!

Notes:

_____
_____
_____
_____
_____
_____
_____
_____

Statement of Belief

If you could only use one sentence to teach this lesson, what would you say?

_____
_____
_____

THREE "R" WORDS

How did we get here?

The American culture struggles with individualism. Why is this a problem?

Discussion Notes

What does God say?

John 1:1-18
Matthew 22:34-40
Acts 2:42-47

Discussion Notes

What can we do?

Three components:
Relocation
Reconciliation
Redistribution

Discussion Notes

How can we do it?

Come up with a measurable, attainable, specific, time-oriented goal (M.A.S.T. goal) that implements the knowledge of these three components into actions

Discussion Notes

"Overflow Church serves the community through multiple efforts... [Overflow] church... supports the local women's safe shelter in practical ways and by loving the people who find safety there... hosts two summer Vacation Bible Schools in areas that are primarily under-resourced, promotes, invites and hosts mission teams to partner with the church to provide practical needs in the community such as home repair and painting neighborhood houses, looks to work with the community and create collaborative efforts and help individuals find places to serve, [and] has a growing street ministry in Benton Harbor."—Overflow Church

Lesson 3—Leader Guide

EARS TO HEAR

Curriculum Goal

Learners will see the importance of the local church deeply rooting themselves into the surrounding community, which will compel the learner to affectively root themselves in relationships with those around them—whether they are a part of the church or not.

Lesson Goals

- The learner will understand the importance of hearing the community's desires
- The learner will understand the main development component
- The learner will challenge themselves in specific ways to listen to the desires of the community

Prep

___ Complete Leader Guide—Use "Instructions for the Leader" as a guide
___ Print one "Learner Guide" for each person
___ Bring writing utensils for learners to use
___ Bring your Bible
___ Pray every day about how God can use you in community development
___ Find a location to meet (coffee shop, house) in the neighborhood near your church
___ Prepare an order for your gathering—Feel free to add worship music, prayer, food, etc.

How did we get here?

Eric and Deanna were parents of an only child—a sixteen-year-old young man named Damon. Eric and Deanna loved Damon with their whole lives. They always tried their best to be good parents. They read every book about parenting that they could get their hands on, went to marriage and family seminars, and frequently took Sunday school classes at church that dealt with parenting. They would give their life to see Damon succeed.

When Damon was in middle school he didn't seem to show much interest in any particular field of study. Eric, being the entrepreneur that he was, decided he would start teaching Damon about good business practices. Damon seemed to be somewhat interested in this, but mainly because he got to spend time with his dad. Eric continued to push Damon to learn more about business, but the more he pushed the more Damon resisted. Eric couldn't figure out what he had done wrong. All he was trying to do was give his son an opportunity to pursue a career path that he had come to love.

At times, our churches can be like Eric, and our community can be like Damon. We can have the greatest of intentions for our community—we can desire for them to succeed—but there is a disconnect. The more we try to help the more we seem to hurt.

What are some of the problems with Eric and Damon's relationship?
Write here...

What does God say?
Read Matthew 20:29-34
What is the problem in this passage?
Write here...

What question does Jesus ask?
Write here...

What can we learn from Jesus in this passage?
Write here...

Read 1 Kings 4:1-7
How does Elisha understand what is going on in the woman's life?
Write here...

What does Elisha ask the woman in V. 2? What are the implications of this?
Write here...

What does Elisha tell the woman to do with the empty vessels? What can we learn from this?
Write here...

What does Elisha tell the woman to do with the full vessels? What can we learn from this?
Write here...

What can we do?
Listening to the Community
Last lesson we talked about three components: Relocation, Reconciliation, and Redistribution. This lesson's component builds off of the first three. In both of these passages we see someone who has a desire and someone who is listening to the desire. The listeners do not see the issue that is at hand and impose what they believe would be the best solution. They simply listen to the desires of the others' hearts. That is the component for this lesson: Listening to the community.

At times, churches have a tendency to impose their will on a community. At times, people have a tendency to impose their will on those they are trying to help. We want to see our neighbors and neighborhood succeed, but we go about it in the wrong way. If we would listen to the desires of our neighbors and neighborhood then we would have a better understand of how we can truly help. Another important aspect of listening is coming to a common answer. It would be wrong to listen to the desires of others and immediately respond with our own answers. Listening to desires also includes helping our neighbors come to a solution for these desires together. We should be helping them walk through the questions and obstacles together; not throwing in our self-imposed "two-cents."

Listening to the community means to listen to the desires of the community, and to help direct the community in ways that they can fulfill their desires.

Briefly summarize listening to the community.
Write here...

How can we do it?

However, It is not enough for us to simply have an understanding of this component. We must be implementing it in our lives. Somehow, we must take what we have learned and make that knowledge a part of what we do. So, how can we do it? How can we listen to the community?

Come up with a measurable, attainable, specific, time-oriented goal (M.A.S.T. goal) that implements the knowledge of this component into actions
Write here...

One Example:
I will invite one family (or single person) who lives within walking distance over to my house for dinner once a week for three months. This person must not be someone that I consider a best friend, or would normally hangout with on the weekends. While having dinner I will intentionally listen for what this person's/family's desires are. If I see that these are healthy desires then I will do my best to ask questions that cause the person/family to think about ways that they can attain their desires. If there are any assets, resources, or connections that I have that can be of help then I will be open to offering them to the person/family as a means to fulfilling their desires. In summary, I will listen to the desires of their heart, and then I will help them find their own way to fulfilling these desires.

What are others saying?

John Perkins is one of the main "gurus" in community development. He started the John Perkins Center, which is where this quote about the importance and implications of listening to the community is found:

> "As we listen to their stories and get to know their hopes and concerns for the present and future, we also begin to identify one another person's deepest felt-needs; those hurts and longings that allows us opportunities to connect with people on a deeper level, which is always necessary for true reconciliation to take place. Listening helps locate the community-based assets. These assets provide a launching pad for self-directed community improvement"

The John Perkins Center reminds us that listening is not something that we "check off" before spouting off our ideas. Listening is about discovering the depths of persons'/communities' desires and then helping them find their own way to fulfilling these desires.

Notes from Pastor/Community Developer

Take everything that you have studied throughout this lesson up to this point and discuss it with a pastor or community developer. These notes may be helpful for understanding and teaching this lesson, so write them down!

Notes:

_____

_____

_____

_____

_____

_____

_____

_____

_____

Notes from Article

Find an article from a magazine, newspaper, online journal, or even a book that relates to the topic of this lesson. These outside sources may offer other insight not received within this curriculum. These notes may be helpful for understanding and teaching this lesson, so write them down!

Notes:

_____

_____

_____

_____

_____

_____

_____

_____

_____

Statement of Belief

If you could only use one sentence to teach this lesson, what would you say?

_____

_____

_____

Lesson 3—Learner Guide
EARS TO HEAR

How did we get here?
At times our churches have the best intentions, but do the wrong things. This is similar to the relationship struggled between Eric and Damon.

Discussion Notes

What does God say?
Matthew 20:29-34
1 Kings 4:1-7

Discussion Notes

What can we do?
One component:
Listening to the Community

Discussion Notes

How can we do it?
Come up with a measurable, attainable, specific, time-oriented goal (M.A.S.T. goal) that implements the knowledge of these three components into actions

Discussion Notes

"As we listen to their stories and get to know their hopes and concerns for the present and future, we also begin to identify one another person's deepest felt-needs; those hurts and longings that allows us opportunities to connect with people on a deeper level, which is always necessary for true reconciliation to take place. Listening helps locate the community-based assets. These assets provide a launching pad for self-directed community improvement"—John Perkins Center

Lesson 4—Leader Guide

Curriculum Goal

Learners will see the importance of the local church deeply rooting themselves into the surrounding community, which will compel the learner to affectively root themselves in relationships with those around them—whether they are a part of the church or not.

Lesson Goals

- The learner will understand the importance of the Church being a sustainable entity that can address wholistic issues—more than just spiritual issues
- The learner will understand the two main development components
- The learner will challenge themselves in specific ways to use their involvement with the community to address wholistic issues with their neighbors

Prep

___ Complete Leader Guide—Use "Instructions for the Leader" as a guide
___ Print one "Learner Guide" for each person
___ Bring writing utensils for learners to use
___ Bring your Bible
___ Pray every day about how God can use you in community development
___ Find a location to meet (coffee shop, house) in the neighborhood near your church
___ Prepare an order for your gathering—Feel free to add worship music, prayer, food, etc.

How did we get here?

During the 1800s, a movement started in Christianity that totally changed the face of ministry within the life of the American church. This movement was fueled by the lack of established homes and churches on the American frontier, and a lack of ordained ministers. The response? Innovative sermons from traveling preachers that held services at outdoor locations for all the people in the area to attend. What did they call this movement? The Camp Meeting movement.

Camp meetings focused heavily upon singing and preaching with mass amounts of people in attendance (though there were times when camp meetings were smaller). Camp meetings mainly targeted those who were lost, and they sought to revive the spiritual life of those in attendance. This movement started a trend of evangelical preaching throughout the American church. If the American church was not focused on the spiritual vitality before, then they were at the time of the Camp Meeting movement.

Our churches still experience the wakes of this wave, today. There are churches and people that focus more on this idea of spiritual vitality and growing closer to God than others. There are churches and people that are more focused on evangelizing the lost than others. However, when these churches and people focus solely on growing closer to God and evangelizing the lost they begin to constrict their focus to two things: 1) Seeking distant and lost people from God, and 2) Seeking to improve the spiritual life of these people.

What are some potential problems with only focusing ministry on distant or lost people?
Write here...

What are some potential problems with only seeking to improve the spiritual life of others in ministry?
Write here...

What does God say?
Read Acts 4:32-37 (Read Acts 4-5 for context)
What was the purpose for selling possessions in this passage?
Write here...

Why would people sell their possessions for the sake of others?

Write here...

Who were the people that were selling the possessions?

Write here...

Read Deuteronomy 6:4-9 (Read Deuteronomy 6 for context)
What is the command that is given by God?

Write here...

Why would God separate heart, soul, and might?

Write here...

How does God desire humanity to love him?

Write here...

What can we do?

As we continue to focus on the 8 Key Components of Christian Community Development it may be apparent that most of these components tend to build off of each other. We have talked about relocation, reconciliation, redistribution, and listening to the community. This lesson's two components are: church-based approach, and wholistic approach.

Church-Based Approach

It is imperative that community development is done within the church. Why? When the church engages with the community they begin a relationship with their neighbors that will, in most cases, be long lasting. The Church is one of the most established institutions in the entire world, and it is not easy for a church to go away in a short period of time. Another reason that a church-based approach to community development is imperative is because this offers a way for spiritual discipleship within the neighborhood. Spiritual discipleship is needed in any Christian organization, and the Church majors in this area.

Wholistic Approach

However, it is important that churches do not focus just on the spiritual and relational aspect. Churches, when rooting themselves in the community, must focus on a wholistic approach to development within the community. This means that they focus on a person's spiritual, physical, emotional, political, cultural, economic, social, moral, judicial, educational, and familial issues. When they focus on all of these issues then they are able to see what affects the person/community as a whole, which enables the church play a part in the long-term development of their neighbors and neighborhood.

Briefly summarize church-based approach and wholistic approach.

Write here...

How can we do it?

However, It is not enough for us to simply have an understanding of these components. We must be implementing them in our lives. Somehow, we must take what we have learned and make that knowledge a part of what we do. So, how can we do it? How can we be church-based and wholistic in our approach?

Come up with a measurable, attainable, specific, time-oriented goal (M.A.S.T. goal) that implements the knowledge of these two components into actions

Write here...

One Example:

I will ask my small group leader to move the small group into a home of a family from church that lives in the community surrounding my church. The focus of the small group will still be largely on digging into the Bible, but once a month we will have a community dinner. This community dinner will be open to anyone living in the surrounding neighborhood. Initially and foundationally the purpose of the dinner will be to dig deep in relationships with people in the neighborhood around the church. After a few months these community dinners will also include a Bible study just like every other week of the small group. During the meal portion of the community dinner the leaders will focus their attention on listening with "wholistic" ears to what is going on in the community member's lives. This will give the small group a chance to help with the wholistic issues of their neighbors. The Bible study will be a chance for the small group to "be the church," and attend to the spiritual and discipleship issues that are going on in the lives of others. This format for small group should last at least one year, but hopefully it will continue one past that first year.

What are others saying?

Shepherd Community Center is an organization that exists to help break the cycle of poverty in Indianapolis, IN. This is part of their wholistic mission for adults, which can be found on their website: shepherdcommunity.org.

> "We will build on these relationships through time and extend our neighbors hope by showing them how to help themselves. We offer benefits assistance, financial planning workshops, job placement, and housing placement; so that they can truly feel helpful and not helpless, hopeful and not hopeless, and joyful not joyless."

Shepherd Community Center reminds us that the relationships we build with the community must involve godly discipleship, but they must also involve addressing the wholistic issues that are present within the community.

Notes from Pastor/Community Developer

Take everything that you have studied throughout this lesson up to this point and discuss it with a pastor or community developer. These notes may be helpful for understanding and teaching this lesson, so write them down!

Notes:

_____

_____

_____

_____

_____

_____

_____

_____

Notes from Article

Find an article from a magazine, newspaper, online journal, or even a book that relates to the topic of this lesson. These outside sources may offer other insight not received within this curriculum. These notes may be helpful for understanding and teaching this lesson, so write them down!

Notes:

_____

_____

_____

_____

_____

_____

_____

_____

Statement of Belief

If you could only use one sentence to teach this lesson, what would you say?

_____

_____

_____

Lesson 4—Learner Guide

MORE THAN SPIRITUAL

How did we get here?

The Camp Meeting Movement emphasized the focus of salvation and holiness. We still see this in our churches today by their targeting distant/lost people, and focusing on their spiritual lives.

What does God say?

Acts 4:32-37
Deuteronomy 6:4-9

What can we do?

Two components:
Church-Based Approach
Wholistic Approach

How can we do it?

Come up with a measurable, attainable, specific, time-oriented goal (M.A.S.T. goal) that implements the knowledge of these three components into actions

Discussion Notes

Discussion Notes

Discussion Notes

Discussion Notes

"We will build on these relationships through time and extend our neighbors hope by showing them how to help themselves. We offer benefits assistance, financial planning workshops, job placement, and housing placement; so that they can truly feel helpful and not helpless, hopeful and not hopeless, and joyful not joyless."—Shepherd Community Center

Lesson 5—Leader Guide

WE HAVE DONE IT OURSELVES!

Curriculum Goal

Learners will see the importance of the local church deeply rooting themselves into the surrounding community, which will compel the learner to affectively root themselves in relationships with those around them—whether they are a part of the church or not.

Lesson Goals

- The learner will understand the importance of developing leaders and empowering others to fulfill their desires—and God's desires
- The learner will understand the two main development components
- The learner will challenge themselves in specific ways to seek opportunities for leadership development and empowerment with their community involvement

Prep

___ Complete Leader Guide—Use "Instructions for the Leader" as a guide
___ Print one "Learner Guide" for each person
___ Bring writing utensils for learners to use
___ Bring your Bible
___ Pray every day about how God can use you in community development
___ Find a location to meet (coffee shop, house) in the neighborhood near your church
___ Prepare an order for your gathering—Feel free to add worship music, prayer, food, etc.

How did we get here?

Year after year they had seen different organizations come and go. They had seen money, temporary jobs, and government projects infiltrate their walls, but they always resulted in the same way: flight. This city in Midwest America was used to people coming in and saying, "We are here for the long-haul." But they never usually stayed in touch with the city for more than a year. Everyone knew that this city needed help. Their average income was below the national poverty line. Their education system relied upon mostly untrained teachers. Their streets were filled with drug and sex trafficking every night of the week. The problem was that nobody knew what to do about it. Organization after organization burnt out with the work that they were trying to do (albeit good work). It wasn't that these outside organizations had bad motives or intentions, but there was something else that was wrong.

What else might have been wrong? Why?
Write here...

What does God say?
Read Nehemiah 2:9-20 (Read Nehemiah 1-2 for context)
In summary, what did Nehemiah do in V. 11-15?
Write here...

What was Nehemiah planning to do in V. 16?
Write here...

What did Nehemiah do in V. 17?
Write here...

What did the workers do in response to Nehemiah's speech in V. 18?
Write here...

Who are the people servants of in V. 20? What are the implications of this?
Write here...

What can we learn about the way that Nehemiah treats the other servants?
Write here...

41

How do you think Nehemiah views the other people?

Write here...

Would the workers have had the courage to rebuild the wall without Nehemiah? Why or why not?

Write here...

What can we do?

So far we have discussed six of the 8 Key Components of Christian Community Development: Relocation, Reconciliation, Redistribution, Listening to the Community, Church-Based Approach, and Wholistic Approach. It is in this scripture passage from Nehemiah that we find the last two components: Leadership Development and Empowerment.

Leadership Development

One of the best things that Nehemiah did at the beginning of his plans to rebuild the wall was find leaders within the community that were capable of completing the work. He walked around the city, and he looked at the places where the wall would be built. While he was doing he was thinking of the perfect people for each spot. He was being strategic about his approach, and he did it in a way that if he were to die the work would have still been brought to completion. The main problem with the opening story to this lesson was that no organization or church was willing to develop leaders within the community. They were only interested in fixing the wound. If a church-based, wholistically minded ministry had sought to find leaders from within the community then they would have been able to make a difference within the community by the strength of those within the community.

Empowerment

Empowerment is the process that sustains leadership development. The goal of empowerment is similar to the goal that children have when raising parents. The goal that parents have for their children is not to meet their every need. The goal that parents have is to help their children find their way into adulthood. In the beginning, the parents tend their child's every need. But as the child matures the parent slowly teaches the child how to be independent when it comes to fulfilling his/her needs. As the child approaches adulthood the parent looks for ways to help their child figure out how to fulfill their good and righteous desires. Then, by the grace of God, the child becomes an adult that is able to empower other individuals (possibly through the 8 Key Components of Christian Community Development). When churches are seeking to empower their neighbors and neighborhood to become an autonomous body they are able to create a sustainable community filled with leadership that is seeking to make the best decisions for the whole group. And together the community can achieve even the highest desire—just like Nehemiah did with the community of Jerusalem.

Briefly summarize leadership development and empowerment.

Write here...

How can we do it?

However, It is not enough for us to simply have an understanding of these components. We must be implementing them in our lives. Somehow, we must take what we have learned and make that knowledge a part of what we do. So, how can we do it? How can we develop leaders and be empowering to those around us?

Come up with a measurable, attainable, specific, time-oriented goal (M.A.S.T. goal) that implements the knowledge of these two components into actions

Write here...

One Example:

I will become a tutor/mentor for one student from the local high school for the remainder of this school year. I will listen to his/her desires, focus on what assets they have, and inspire him/her to be a leader in the ways that best fit who he/she is. I won't just focus on developing him/her as a leader for this school year, but I will intentionally help the student find their own way to achieving greater things in the future. This could be empowering him/her to be the first person in their family to make it to college. By empowering him/her to passionately pursue his/her desires, and by developing him/her as a leader there is a great chance that this person will continue to develop and empower other people in the future. Along with leadership development and empowerment I hope to disciple this person in the character of God. Seeing the true character of God is just as important as being empowered and developed as a leader.

What are others saying?

There is a famous poem that is circulating through the community development field. It is an ancient Chinese proverb, but has been made most famous by the Christian Community Development Association. It says:

Go to the people
Live among them
Learn from them
Love them
Start with what they know
Build on what they have
But of the best of leaders
When their task is done
The people will remark
"We have done it ourselves."
-Ancient Chinese Proverb

This poem captures the true essence of community development. From the beginning of this study on the 8 Key Components of Christian Community Development (relocating) all the way to the end (empowering) one can see that the goal of community development is not to be another leader and force among the people, but the goal is to be a Christlike servant.

Notes from Pastor/Community Developer

Take everything that you have studied throughout this lesson up to this point and discuss it with a pastor or community developer. These notes may be helpful for understanding and teaching this lesson, so write them down!

Notes:

_____

_____

_____

_____

_____

_____

_____

_____

Notes from Article

Find an article from a magazine, newspaper, online journal, or even a book that relates to the topic of this lesson. These outside sources may offer other insight not received within this curriculum. These notes may be helpful for understanding and teaching this lesson, so write them down!

Notes:

_____

_____

_____

_____

_____

_____

_____

_____

Statement of Belief

If you could only use one sentence to teach this lesson, what would you say?

_____

_____

_____

WE HAVE DONE IT OURSELVES!

How did we get here?
Organizations, at times, try to move into cities to develop the communities, but many times the end up leaving quickly. Why is this?

What does God say?
Nehemiah 2:9-20

What can we do?
Two components:
Leadership Development
Empowerment

How can we do it?
Come up with a measurable, attainable, specific, time-oriented goal (M.A.S.T. goal) that implements the knowledge of these three components into actions

"Go to the people... Live among them... Learn from them... Love them... Start with what they know... Build on what they have... But of the best of leaders... When their task is done... The people will remark: 'We have done it ourselves.'"—Ancient Chinese Proverb

Lesson 6—Leader Guide

Curriculum Goal

Learners will see the importance of the local church deeply rooting themselves into the surrounding community, which will compel the learner to affectively root themselves in relationships with those around them—whether they are a part of the church or not.

Lesson Goals

- The learner will understand how to channel the understand and knowledge received throughout this curriculum into effective actions
- The learner will assemble a church-wide initiative based off of the 8 Key Components of Christian Community Development

Prep

___ Complete Leader Guide—Use "Instructions for the Leader" as a guide
___ Print one "Learner Guide" for each person
___ Bring writing utensils for learners to use
___ Bring your Bible
___ Pray every day about how God can use you in community development
___ Find a location to meet (coffee shop, house) in the neighborhood near your church
___ Prepare an order for your gathering—Feel free to add worship music, prayer, food, etc.

What do we do now?

We have now walked through all 8 Key Components of Christian Community Development. These components are a way for churches to step into their surrounding neighborhoods and bring healing to the community. So what is next?

Learning these components will mean nothing if they are not translated into action. All throughout these lessons we have been setting MAST goals for ourselves. These have been measurable, attainable, specific, and time-oriented goals that have related to the components that each lesson covered. Now, it is time to set a MAST goal for our church.

How can we do it?

For the remainder of this lesson, we will be setting a MAST goal for our church. There are four qualifications for this goal:

- **Long-Term**: This goal should not be focused on one single event; rather it should be focused on a continual, long-term, consistent action. Christian Community Development cannot be done in one week, or sometimes even one year.
- **All of the 8 Key Components must be utilized in some way**: Using just one of the key components is a good start, but the key to Christian Community Development is combine multiple layers of the 8 Key Components.
- **Away from church grounds**: This implies that the first key component, relocation, will be used.
- **Church leadership team meeting**: When finished with designing the MAST goal for the church, set up a meeting with the church leadership team to discuss how to tangibly meet this goal as a church body.

Guideline for Christian Community Development Action

Use this guideline to help point you in the right direction for coming up with a MAST goal:

- **Where does the church focus its attention in ministry?**
  Write here...

- **What barriers are between the church and the surrounding neighborhood?**
  Write here...

- **What are some voiced desires of the surrounding neighborhood?**
  Write here...

- **What are some assets/resources that the surrounding neighborhood possesses?**
  Write here...

- Are there any leaders in the surrounding neighborhood? Are there individuals who could potentially be leaders?

  Write here…

- How can the church effectively be a part of this surrounding neighborhood?

  Write here…

Come up with a measurable, attainable, specific, time-oriented goal (M.A.S.T. goal) for the church to participate in Christian Community Development.

Write here…

Notes from Pastor/Community Developer

Take everything that you have studied throughout this lesson up to this point and discuss it with a pastor or community developer. These notes may be helpful for understanding and teaching this lesson, so write them down!

Notes:

_____

_____

_____

_____

_____

_____

_____

_____

Notes from Article

Find an article from a magazine, newspaper, online journal, or even a book that relates to the topic of this lesson. These outside sources may offer other insight not received within this curriculum. These notes may be helpful for understanding and teaching this lesson, so write them down!

Notes:

_____

_____

_____

_____

_____

_____

_____

_____

Statement of Belief

If you could only use one sentence to teach this lesson, what would you say?

_____

_____

_____

Lesson 6—Learner Guide
GO LIVE IT!

How can we do it?
4 Qualifications for the church-wide MAST goal:
- **Long-term**
- **All of the 8 Key Components must be utilized in some way**
- **Away from church grounds**
- **Church leadership team meeting**

Guideline for Christian Community Development Action
Use this guideline to help point you in the right direction for coming up with a MAST goal:
- **Where does the church focus its attention in ministry?**
  Write here...

- **What barriers are between the church and the surrounding neighborhood?**
  Write here...

- **What are some voiced desires of the surrounding neighborhood?**
  Write here...

- **What are some assets/resources that the surrounding neighborhood possesses?**
  Write here...

- **Are there any leaders in the surrounding neighborhood? Are there individuals who could potentially be leaders?**
  Write here...

- **How can the church effectively be a part of this surrounding neighborhood?**
  Write here...

On the back of this sheet come up with a measurable, attainable, specific, time-oriented goal (M.A.S.T. goal) for the church to participate in Christian Community Development.

RESOURCES USED:

8 Key Components of Christian Community Development (Christian Community Development Association—ccda.org)

Christian Community Development Association (ccda.org)

Ancient Chinese Proverb (ccda.org)

Shepherd Community Center (shepherdcommunity.org)

Overflow Church (overflowchurch.org)

John Perkins Center (perkinscenter.blogspot.com)

An Introduction to Community Development—Edited by Rhonda Phillips and Robert H. Pittman

The Holy Bible, English Standard Version® (ESV®)
Copyright © 2001 by Crossway,
a publishing ministry of Good News Publishers.
All rights reserved.
ESV Text Edition: 2007

13957429R00032

Made in the USA
Lexington, KY
29 February 2012